D1031881

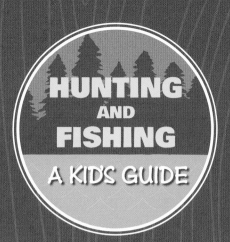

**HUNTING AND FISHING**

**A KID'S GUIDE**

# We're Going
# DEER
# HUNTING

Shelby Moran

**PowerKiDS**
press.

New York

Published in 2017 by The Rosen Publishing Group, Inc.
29 East 21st Street, New York, NY 10010

First Edition

Editor: Melissa Raé Shofner
Book Design: Tanya Dellaccio

Photo Credits: Cover, p.5 Tom Reichner/Shutterstock.com; all pages except p. 2 (wood texture) sittipong/Shutterstock.com; back cover, pp. 1, 3–4, 6–8, 10–12, 14–16, 18, 20–22, 24, 26–28, 30–32 (background) ArtBitz/Shutterstock.com; p. 7 (moose) Menno Schaefer; p. 7 (elk) Paul Staniszewski/Shutterstock.com; p. 7 (caribou) Jeff McGraw/ Shutterstock.com; p. 9 Jeff Feverston/Shutterstock.com; p. 11 (whitetail deer) Bruce MacQueen/Shutterstock.com; p. 11 (mule deer) Robert Postma/Design Pics/Getty Images; p. 13 Fuse/Corbis/Getty Images; p. 14 Guy J. Sagi/Shutterstock.com; p. 15 (hunter) William Campbell/Corbis News/Getty Images; p. 15 (deer tracks) Mike Vande Ven Jr/Shutterstock.com; p. 16 AlissalaKerr/Shutterstock.com; p. 17 (female hunter) Johner Images/Getty Images; p. 17 (male hunter) Dmitry Kalinovsky/ Shutterstock.com; p. 18 chris kolaczan/Shutterstock.com; p. 19 9387388673/Shutterstock.com; p. 20 Jeffrey B. Banke/ Shutterstock.com; p. 21 (hunting stand) berczy04/Shutterstock.com; p. 21 (trail) Andrew Sabai/Shutterstock.com; p. 23 Terry Schmidbauer/Getty Images; p. 25 Nate Allred/Shutterstock.com; p. 27 (ammo holder) iofoto/Shutterstock.com; p. 27 (scope) welcomia/Shutterstock.com; p. 29 Tyler Stableford/Getty Images; p. 30 Nate Allred/Shutterstock.com.

Cataloging-in-Publication Data

Names: Moran, Shelby.
Title: We're going deer hunting / Shelby Moran.
Description: New York : PowerKids Press, 2017. | Series: Hunting and fishing: a kid's guide | Includes index.
Identifiers: ISBN 9781499427509 (pbk.) | ISBN 9781499428759 (library bound) | ISBN 9781508152804 (6 pack)
Subjects: LCSH: Deer hunting–Juvenile literature.
Classification: LCC SK301.M67 2017 | DDC 799.2'765–dc23

Manufactured in the United States of America

CPSIA Compliance Information: Batch #BW17PK: For Further Information contact Rosen Publishing, New York, New York at 1-800-237-9932

# CONTENTS

# THE HISTORY OF DEER HUNTING

Deer are some of the most hunted animals in North America. Deer hunting has a long history here. Deer were valuable to Native Americans because just one deer could provide a lot of meat. Deer also provided skin and fur for clothing and shelter. Their **antlers** were used to make tools.

Today, people hunt deer for sport. Deer hunting remains a popular hobby in the United States. Some people take off from work or school to celebrate the first day of **rifle** season.

## HUNTING HINT

Deer meat is called venison.

Male deer are called bucks, bulls, or stags.

# THE DEER FAMILY

In addition to the deer most people hunt, the deer family also includes other big-game animals such as elk, caribou, and moose. The males of this family all have antlers. These are sometimes called horns. However, horns last a lifetime, while antlers fall off in winter or early spring. The males grow new antlers each year.

Have you ever seen antlers hanging on a wall? They make great **trophies**—especially big antler racks with lots of points. You can count the number of branches on a deer's rack to figure out how many points it has.

## HUNTING HINT

Male deer use their antlers to fight over which ones will get to mate, or make babies, with females.

Antlers are made of bone. They have a soft covering while they're growing.

moose

elk

caribou

# COMMON DEER SPECIES

White-tailed deer are the most commonly hunted animals in the United States. This species, or kind, of deer can be found in almost every state. They also live in Canada and South America. Whitetails can weigh up to 220 pounds (99.8 kg).

White-tailed deer and mule deer look very similar, but mule deer are slightly larger. These deer live in western states, such as Colorado. They can weigh up to 250 pounds (113.4 kg). If you shoot a mule deer or a whitetail, you might need some help dragging it out of the woods.

## HUNTING HINT

The white-tailed deer is the official state animal of several states, including Pennsylvania.

White-tailed deer are very common in mid-Atlantic states, such as Pennsylvania, Virginia, and West Virginia. In fact, they're sometimes called Virginia deer.

# FINDING A DEER

Deer have many different kinds of **habitats**. They can be found in forests, fields, swamps, and farm country. That means people can hunt in many different kinds of surroundings. Many people prefer hunting in the woods because they can hide in the trees.

Deer are most active around sunrise and sunset. It's a smart idea to be in your deer-hunting spot before the sun is up. Shoot only if there is enough light to see, though. You want to be able to see the deer clearly!

This deer is standing in a meadow as the sun is rising.

## HUNTING HINT

In the summer, deer often hide in the forest because the shade keeps them cool.

# THE BEST COLOR

Deer hunters often wear the color orange. Most states require hunters to wear bright orange so other hunters can see them.

Deer can't see colors the same way humans do. While deer don't recognize orange, they do see patterns. Hunters often wear **camouflage** patterns to blend in. Some states have **archery** seasons that permit hunters to go without wearing orange. However, this is only allowed when that season doesn't overlap with other seasons, such as turkey season. The turkey hunters might be using guns!

## HUNTING HINT

This shade of bright orange is called blaze orange or hunter orange.

It's important to wear orange, even if you're bowhunting. It's risky to hunt if you can't be seen by other hunters.

13

# DEER-HUNTING CHALLENGES

Many people hunt deer because it's a challenge. Deer have great **defenses**. They have excellent senses of sight, hearing, and smell. They're also very fast, which means they're hard to shoot once their senses warn them of danger.

Deer are big animals. It takes a powerful weapon to kill them. Most deer hunters use rifles. These are long firearms that are held tightly against the shoulder. Rifles fire long, thin bullets that travel far and cause great harm to their targets.

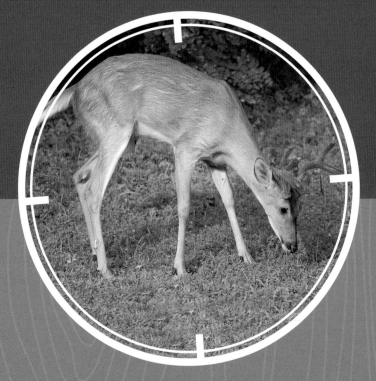

Many hunters look around to find deer prints to track deer. Before you set out on a hunt, learn the tracks of the animals that live nearby.

## HUNTING HINT

Hunters can purchase special scents to mask their own smells and draw deer to them.

deer tracks

# GREAT SHOT!

Many deer hunters use rifles. However, certain kinds of rifles are outlawed in several states. It's unsafe to hunt with rifles near communities. This is where shotguns come in handy.

Unlike rifles, shotguns aren't made to shoot single bullets. Instead, they scatter small pellets called shot. It's also possible to load shotguns with single shells called slugs. Slugs don't travel as far as bullets, but they do more harm than shot. They can kill a deer, while shot would just wound it.

shotgun slugs

## HUNTING HINT

If you hunt deer with a shotgun, make sure it's loaded with slugs. It's against the law to hunt deer with shot because it may cause the deer pain without killing it.

Rifles fire single bullets. Hunters looking for greater **accuracy** should use a rifle. Shotguns shoot slugs or scatter shot, which can spread out over a large area.

rifle

shotgun

17

# ARCHERY SEASON

Want an even greater challenge? Some deer hunters choose to hunt during archery season. This is a special season when hunters may hunt only with bows. Archery is one of the oldest forms of hunting. Newer **compound** bows can shoot farther and with more accuracy than the simple ones used in the past.

Even with these new bows, archery is not easy. Bowhunters must be able to get closer to deer than hunters using rifles and shotguns. They rely on camouflage and scents in order to do this.

broadhead

## HUNTING HINT

Archery hunters use arrowheads called broadheads that are made especially for hunting deer.

Compound bows have more parts than simple bows.

# SILENCE IS GOLDEN

There are several methods for successful hunting. However, each one requires the hunter to be as quiet as possible.

One method is to find a good spot and sit there patiently. How can you tell if a spot is good? Look for deer tracks and game trails. Some hunters sit in tree stands, which are **platforms** in or near trees. They offer good views of the area. Hunters often hunt with blinds, or screens that hide them from deer.

You might have to wait a while for deer, but it's important to stay quiet the whole time.

# HUNTING HINT

Game trails are small paths that animals use when traveling through an area.

# STALKING DEER

Some deer hunters would rather be more active while hunting. Another method is to stalk, or still-hunt, deer. This is the art of moving slowly, carefully, and quietly through the woods. It requires hunters to pay attention to their surroundings. They can't wear clothing that makes noise. They keep their eyes open for animal tracks.

Snow can play an important role in hunting, whether for good or for bad. Animal tracks can be easy to see in the snow, but a fresh snowfall will hide them.

## HUNTING HINT

If you can, explore the area where you want to hunt before you actually hunt there.

Can you move through a room without anyone noticing? You might be good at still-hunting someday!

23

# PREPARING FOR THE HUNT

Are you ready to go deer hunting? First, you must have a hunting **license** that proves you've passed your state's firearm safety program. Most deer hunters wear their license pinned to the back of their jacket. Each state has different hunting laws, so make sure you know the rules for your state.

Practice your shooting before the hunting season begins. This is especially important when using a new gun. Many sporting clubs have shooting ranges. There, you can practice shooting from different positions.

## HUNTING HINT

States have different laws about the age at which a person can start hunting. Often, kids can go along with an adult while they hunt and learn all about the sport.

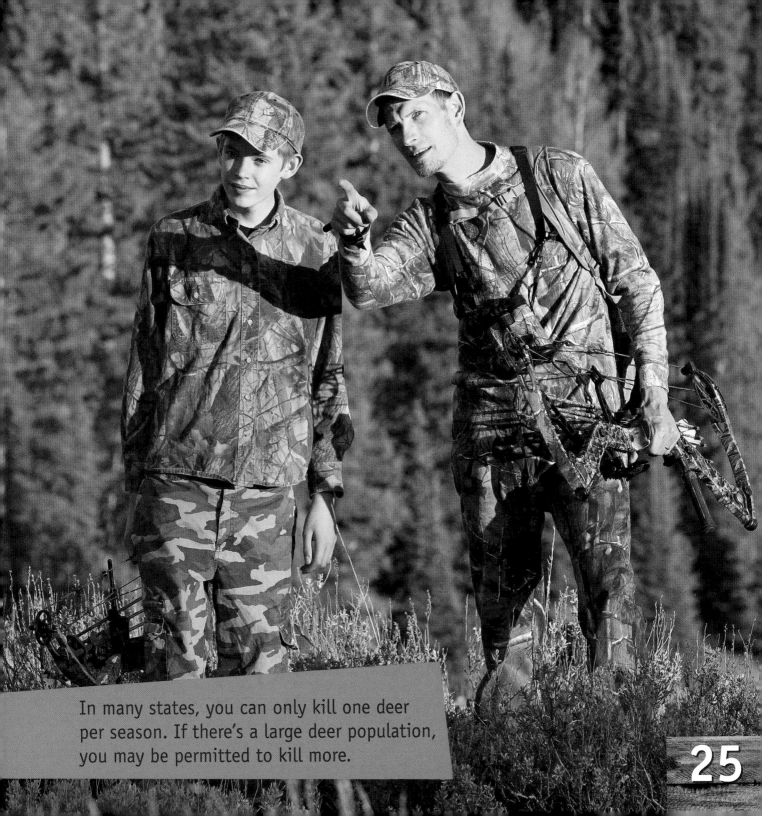

In many states, you can only kill one deer per season. If there's a large deer population, you may be permitted to kill more.

# THE SECRET TO GREAT AIM

Scopes are tools that **magnify** faraway objects. They have crosshairs, or targets, to help you aim. Many hunters use scopes on their rifles. Good hunters try to kill deer as cleanly as possible. They don't want animals to suffer.

You will need to "sight in" your rifle before taking it hunting. This makes sure that your rifle and scope are aiming at the same spot. If you need help sighting in your rifle, ask an adult or check the instructions that came with the scope.

Scopes are one of your best tools for learning how to aim correctly.

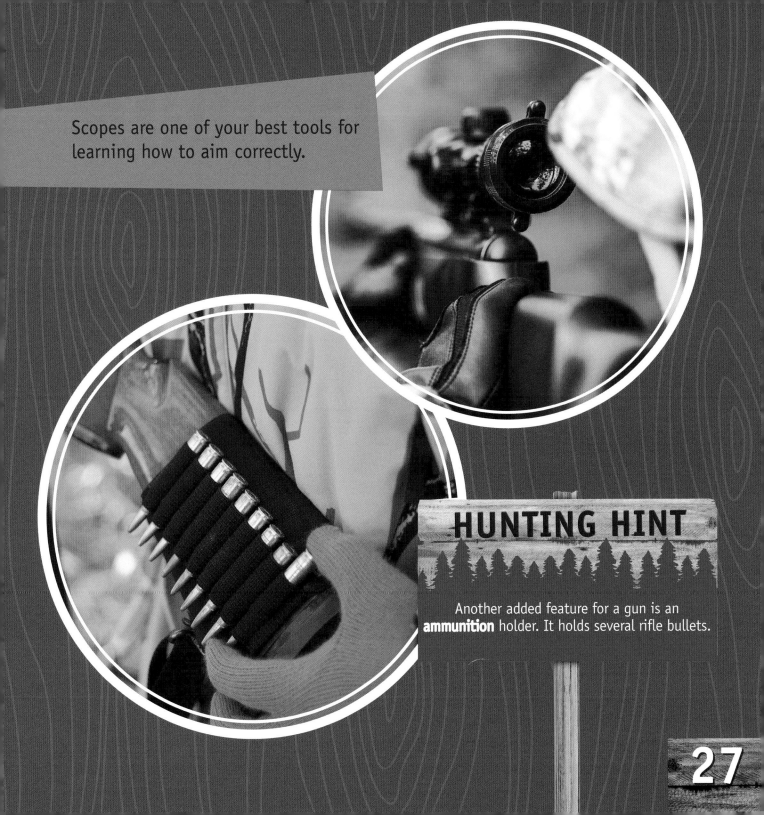

## HUNTING HINT

Another added feature for a gun is an **ammunition** holder. It holds several rifle bullets.

# AFTER THE HUNT

If you follow the rules of deer hunting and practice safety, you may shoot your very own deer! However, your work isn't done. The first thing you must do is tag your deer. The tag is a form on your license. Fill out the form and put it on your deer.

Next you must field dress, or clean, your kill so the meat doesn't spoil. To clean a deer, you'll need a sharp knife, rope, plastic gloves, and garbage bags.

## HUNTING HINT

Some butchers specialize in preparing deer meat. They can make venison steaks, jerky, and even ground venison for hamburgers.

This buck's rack would make a great trophy. Can you count how many points it has?

# NATURE'S BALANCE

Can hunting actually help deer? In many places, deer have few natural predators. This leads to deer populations that are so large there's not enough food to go around. Large deer populations also create unsafe driving conditions. Many deer are killed by cars. You've probably seen the bodies of these deer on the side of the road.

Deer hunters play an important part in **ecosystems** by controlling deer populations. The government sometimes hires hunters when population levels get too high. **Responsible** deer hunters help keep nature in balance!

# GLOSSARY

**accuracy:** The ability to hit the intended target.
**ammunition:** Bullets, shells, and other things fired by weapons.
**antlers:** The pair of horns on a deer, moose, or elk.
**archery:** The activity of shooting with a bow and arrow.
**camouflage:** A clothing pattern that soldiers and hunters wear to make them harder to see.
**compound:** Made up of two or more parts.
**defense:** A feature of a living thing that helps keep it safe.
**ecosystem:** All the living things in an area.
**habitat:** The natural home for plants, animals, and other living things.
**license:** An official paper giving someone the right to do something.
**magnify:** To make something appear larger.
**platform:** A flat surface that's raised higher than the ground.
**rifle:** A gun with a long part called a barrel. It's held against your shoulder when you shoot it.
**responsible:** Able to choose for oneself what is right; showing care for things you have to do.
**trophy:** An object that can be displayed to show one's skill or success.

# INDEX

# WEBSITES